O. C. Dalhouse Ross

Spain and the War with Morocco

O. C. Dalhouse Ross

Spain and the War with Morocco

ISBN/EAN: 9783337013196

Printed in Europe, USA, Canada, Australia, Japan

Cover: Foto ©ninafisch / pixelio.de

More available books at **www.hansebooks.com**

SPAIN

AND THE

,/AR WITH MOROCCO.

BY

O. C. DALHOUSIE ROSS, ESQ.

A RESIDENT IN SPAIN FOR MANY YEARS.

General O'Donnell's Speech in the Cortes, explaining the causes of
the outbreak of hostilities.
Great enthusiasm throughout the country. Patriotic offers from
all classes. Anecdote of Cuchares the Bull-fighter.
The question of Coupons examined and explained.
Description of the Spanish possessions on the Coast of Morocco.
Ceuta, El Peñon, Melilla and Alhucema.
Outrages committed by the Riff Pirates.
Reasons for the popularity of the war. Speech of the Marquis of
Molins in the Senate.
Spain's desire to be " respected abroad and united at home."
Account of O'Donnell's Pronunciamento and the Revolution of 1854.
Anecdotes of the Revolution.
Fall of Espartero in 1856. State of parties in Spain.
" Union-Liberal."
Present highly prosperous state of the country. Education, rail-
ways, commerce, revenue compared with that of other coun-
tries, Army and Navy. *Desamortizacion.*
Introduction of Christianity and civilization into Africa.
The war not undertaken at the instigation of France.

LONDON:
JAMES RIDGWAY, PICCADILLY. W.
1860.

Price One Shilling.

SPAIN AND THE WAR WITH MOROCCO.

On the 22nd of October it was announced to the Spanish Cortes that the Government had determined on declaring war with Morocco.

In a plain and lucid speech, Marshal O'Donnell, the President of the Council of Ministers, related to the Congress the immediate causes of the outbreak of hostilities in the following terms :

" After the words that I yesterday had the honour of addressing to the Congress, I think that every gentleman now present must be prepared to hear, without surprise, the grave information which the Government has to communicate. Not only are our relations with Morocco interrupted, but the Government considers that the time has arrived when it becomes necessary to make an appeal to arms, in order to enforce . . . (here a general explosion of applause and *vivas* drowned the Minister's voice, making it for several minutes impossible for him to proceed. He then resumed) . . . in order to enforce satisfaction for the insults that have been offered to the Spanish nation, and to secure this country against a repetition of such proceedings as those which I am about to communicate to the Congress : for the Government is of opinion that, besides the written documents which the constitution requires should be presented to the Cortes explanatory of our motives for declaring war, it is advisable that a short statement be made describing the whole course of the negociations.

"Our relations with the Empire of Morocco, in connection with our possessions in Africa, are of two sorts, the first having reference to the fortress of Ceuta, the second to the prison establishments of Alhucema, Melilla and El Peñon. By our treaties with the Emperor of Morocco, he is not to be held responsible for any attacks that may be made on the three last named places by the half-savage tribes which surround them, and the expression used in these treaties is that Spain herself is authorised to repel every sort of aggression on the part of the Moors with " mortars and cannon."

" But at Ceuta, in virtue of the treaty of 1845, which fixed the limits of the fortress, and the extent of the neutral ground, a Moroccan officer has been placed in authority on the spot, and provided with a guard of what are there called *moros de rey* (King's Moors) and to him is intrusted the protection of the garrison of our fortress from any act of outward aggression. This position has been maintained ever since 1845; our relations with Morocco, with respect to the fortress have been friendly, and we have not had to deplore any serious misunderstanding. But in the month of August last, some Moors, either a portion of those on guard, or some whom the guard allowed to approach, invaded our territory and overthrew the stone pillar bearing the arms of Spain, which formed the limit of the Moorish and Spanish camps.

"The governor of Ceuta on the following morning conferred with the officer in command of the Serrallo, who made apologies for the act, and the Governor was content to report the circumstance to our Consul at Tangiers and to Her Majesty's government.

"The same day, however, other hostile acts were committed, and our sentinels on the boundaries between the two camps, were fired upon. Again, a few days later, between five and six hundred Moors attacked the troops forming our garrison, who, thereupon sallied forth, and in defence of our territory drove them back as far as the boundary line; but our soldiers were then again fired upon, and this constituted a still more serious act of aggression.

"When the Government learnt what had passed, instructions were sent to our Consul, and *chargé d'affaires* at Tangiers, desiring him to inform the Sultan's minister, that the Spanish Government could on no account tolerate the insults and aggressions which had just been committed, that we believed, or desired to believe, that they had not been sanctioned by the Sultan, and that accordingly prompt satisfaction was expected. We required that the Spanish arms should be replaced by the Moors, that the Spanish flag should be saluted by the authorities, and that the offending parties should receive punishment before the walls of Ceuta, and in presence of the Moroccan authorities.

"The reply of the Minister of the Sultan was completely satisfactory : he said that he was ready to give us the satisfaction that we demanded, that he would instantly make the necessary arrangements to have the offending parties arrested, and that he would do this, notwithstanding his belief that the garrison of Ceuta had occasioned the offence to be committed, by coming out of the fortress in pursuit of the Moors.

"Such an excuse, the Congress will understand was inadmissible, for it would be contrary to common sense, if the garrison were unable to issue from the fortress within the limits of its own territory, and to maintain such a thing would be to deny that we are the owners of the ground, which has been assigned to us by treaty, and the boundaries of which are marked by stone pillars bearing the arms of Spain.

"In the instructions which were sent to the *chargé d'affaires* of Spain, he was told that reparation must be obtained within a term of ten days, and if refused, that he must withdraw. Just at this moment, however, the Emperor of Morocco died, and his Minister, whilst still assuring us that he was ready to give the satisfaction we required, drew our attention to the state of the kingdom, and the expediency of first allowing the new Government to be firmly established, as difficulties are always created in that kingdom by a change of sovereigns.

"The Spanish Government, which only desired

that justice should be done, and only required proper satisfaction for insults that had been offered to our flag, wishing to give a fresh proof of its moderation, although placing but little faith in the sincerity of the Moroccans, consented to a further delay of 20 days. During this time, after this term had been fixed, the attacks on the Ceuta garrison, far from ceasing, were repeated on a more formidable scale, and two combats took place between the Moors and the battalions of the *chasseurs* who had recently arrived at Ceuta, combats in which Spanish blood was shed and several of our men were wounded : such an act of aggression was of the most grave description, and naturally the reparation required by this country had to be increased in the same proportion as the offence had risen in magnitude.

" The Moroccans again requested a further term of nine days, again acknowledging our right to demand satisfaction, and assuring us of their readiness to comply with it. A third delay was granted, on condition, however, that guarantees for the future should be given us, and in the diplomatic note which was passed on this occasion, besides requiring reparation for the offences that had been given, it was stated that one of the conditions required by us was the cession of a space of ground sufficient in extent to give as it were breathing room and security to the garrison.

" On the 13th, two days before the expiration of the last term that had been fixed, the Minister of the Sultan represented to us that he had full powers from the Emperor to bring the question then pending with Spain to a conclusion, that he accepted in principle all that we asked, and that the extension of Ceuta should be conceded as far as the heights required for the security of the fortress and breathing room for the garrison of Ceuta.

"This being the case, the Government, believing that it was really intended to conclude the settlement of the questions then pending, fixed the terms of the arrangement as follows:

"Satisfaction for the offence: the Pasha of Tangiers and Tetuan to come before Ceuta, and in his presence the arms of Spain to be replaced on the same spot from whence they were removed. Moorish troops to accompany the Pasha and to salute the Spanish flag as a reparation for the insults that had been offered to it; the persons who had committed the offence and who ought to be known to the Morocco government, to be brought before the fortress of Ceuta in order that they might be punished on the spot where the blood of Spaniards had been shed. We were, moreover, as moderate as possible on the question of boundary. Being convinced that it was necessary to mark certain heights and other points, we proposed to the Sultan that he should name two Commissioners and we on our side would name two engineers in order that the new boundary line should be fixed by mutual agreement, the Sierra de Bullones being taken as the basis thereof; but as the Sierra is very extensive, it was added that only a portion of it should be included and a proper limit fixed by the Commissioners.

"Everything having been thus settled on such reasonable terms, the Congress will understand with what astonishment Her Majesty's Government now received a communication from the Minister, in which it was stated, not that we required too much, but that he had not sufficient powers to conclude this negociation; that he must consult with the Emperor who would decide! What could we answer to this, when every sort of consideration and so much regard to their representations had already been shown by us? Could it be expected that we should grant a further delay to the Government of Morocco? No, gentlemen, this was impossible, our dignity, even the honour of our country forbad it, for we had already given proofs of the greatest moderation in consenting so often to an extension of the term, and also in not taking advantage of the unsettled state of the Sultan's dominions—and this is moreover an answer to those who have supposed that a spirit of conquest and not a just demand for reparation, takes us to Africa.

"Our *chargé d'affaires* was accordingly informed that in consequence of this communication, in which there were many inaccurate statements, he must immediately break off his diplomatic relations with Morocco, and that the fortune of war should now decide between us—war which is the last argument of Kings and of Nations.

" We come, therefore, full of confidence to declare
everything to the Congress, feeling convinced that
the Government has acted throughout with the
moderation and the temperate spirit which becomes
a people which is still a great nation, although the
contrary may by some be believed ; of a people
which possesses the means of enforcing respect, and
which is determined ever to hold its honour and its
dignity as high as they are held by the proudest of
nations.

" It is not a spirit of conquest which animates us ;
no. The God of Battles will bless our arms, and
the valour of our troops and of our navy will prove
to the Moroccans that Spain is not to be insulted with
impunity, and that we are determined to obtain reparation, even should we have to seek it on their
hearth stones.

" I repeat it is not a spirit of conquest which takes
us to Africa, neither shall European interests suffer
in the least degree by our expedition; no ! No
thought of the kind enters our minds ; we go thither
to redeem our honour, to require guarantees for the
future, we go to enforce from the Moroccans an in-
demnity for all that we have suffered ; in one word,
with our arms in our hands, we go to require satisfaction for the insults offered to our flag. No one
can charge us with ambition, no one can with reason
complain of our conduct. We are strong in our
right and our motives are irreproachable, the rest is
in the hands of the God of Battles !"

This speech was followed by vehement and prolonged applause from all parts of the House, the cheers from the deputies inside the building were echoed by an enthusiastic crowd in the streets outside, and the welcome news that war had been declared flew rapidly to every part of the city. At night the houses were spontaneously illuminated, and a feeling of intense satisfaction was evident in the whole population of Madrid. On this subject all classes and all parties seem to be for the first time unanimous. The speakers in the Congress who followed General O'Donnell were the leaders of different parties most in opposition to the Government, Calvo Asensio, Olozoga, Gonzalez Bravo, yet all spoke in terms of the highest approbation of the war; and the first named, who is the proprietor of the liberal paper the "*Iberia,*" presented a memorial from the representatives of the whole of the Madrid press, eulogising the conduct of the Government, and promising their unanimous support as long as the war should last.

Throughout the whole of Spain the news has had the same effect, and everywhere an enthusiasm reigns which it is difficult to describe.

Volunteers enrol themselves in all directions, and private subscriptions flow in on a scale that has never before been known. The city of Barcelona offers to supply a battalion of 700 men, a brigade of mules and everything necessary for a hospital; the princely Duke of Osuna undertakes to raise and equip at his own expense a battalion of 700 men, and to maintain them until the conclusion of the war, and many other private individuals have offered to do the same with a smaller number. Manzanedo, a Madrid capitalist, besides equipping and maintaining 100 men, lends the sum of £20,000 to the treasury without interest for the same period, whilst a bank at Barcelona supplies, on the same terms, the sum of £50,000, and the Basque provinces £40,000 and 3000 soldiers.

The Queen herself magnanimously proposes that if money be wanted her private lands and her jewels should be sold : "if it be necessary," she is said to have exclaimed at the last Council of Ministers which preceded the declaration of war, " let all the " expenses of my palace be diminished, a simple " ribbon will become me better than diamond neck- " laces, if my jewels can supply the means of restor- " ing the fame of my country !"

Ladies volunteer their services for the hospitals, the clergy unanimously refuse the exemption from the war-tax which was proposed in the law presented to the Cortes, *employés* give up their pay to the Government for the time that the war may last, and lastly (perhaps this is not the least curious illustration of the complete unanimity throughout the country) the Spanish papers announce that the *celebre matador*, Cuchares* has contributed large numbers

* The answer of this man to an inquiry whether he would give his services gratuitously in a bull-fight to be held at Seville, in aid of the fund for the relief of the wounded, was characteristic. He

of oxen and sheep to aid in the maintenance of the expeditionary army.

The spectacle of so much patriotism could not fail to kindle some sympathy in England were it not that the object of the war is almost entirely ignored in this country ; it is scarcely known in England that a war between Spain and Morocco has been for a long time impending, few people understand the cause of quarrel, and with some even an impression prevails that Spain is acting but as the tool of France, or at any rate that she must soon become so. Perhaps it is this impression which has been one of the chief causes of the unpleasant spirit that has been manifested towards Spain on this occasion by a part of the English press; but there is no doubt also that at the present moment a generally unfriendly feeling exists in this country towards everything Spanish, occasioned probably in a great measure by the very imperfect knowledge which prevails of the modern history and the present state of the Peninsula, and partly also there can be no doubt, by the sort of mercantile hostility which has existed for the last few years between the two countries, in consequence of the unsatisfactory arrangement which was entered into by Spain when attempting to settle the so long pending question of overdue *Coupons*.

So much importance has been attached to this

replied by telegraph from Trujillo : " In such a cause I am ready " to give all that I possess, and to kill all the bulls in Spain, and " have no doubt the owners of bulls will be equally patriotic."

subject in England that the outbreak of a war, brought on in a great measure by her chivalrous desire once for all to put an end to the troublesome pirates who are the scourge of that part of the Mediterranean, has only given rise to numberless attacks in the public press on her honesty and financial credit.

The general impression which exists in this country with reference to the *Coupons* is, however, in a great measure founded on misconception, and it is but fair to Spain to say that the light in which the question is regarded by the two countries is quite dissimilar.

In England she is charged with being a "repudiating state," and no epithet is considered too strong to brand her conduct towards the coupons holders. But in Spain the fact of her having been guilty of *repudiation* is utterly denied, and nothing is more offensive to a Spaniard than to hear such a charge made against his country.

The facts of the case may, we believe, be stated in a few words :—

The finances of Spain were brought into an almost hopeless condition by a seven years' desolating civil war, which followed a reign distinguished by a series of great misfortunes, by the loss of her magnificent colonies, and by an iniquitous French invasion to suppress the first Liberal government that her people had endeavoured to establish.

In 1831, shortly before the outbreak of this civil

war—in which Englishmen and Spaniards fought
side by side in the cause of liberty—some foreign
loans had been contracted, upon which the interest
was duly paid until 1840, but from that time remained unsettled for a period of eleven years,
literally because the conflict between the rival parties
had exhausted the revenues of the country. With
the triumph of Liberal institutions, however, Spain
also conquered an amount of material prosperity to
which for many years she had been a stranger, and
in 1851 she was able again to resume payment on
the loans in question.

She could not pay in full all the arrears of interest
that had accumulated, for by that time they exceeded the amount of the original capital. But,
it is maintained by her that she did all that she
could, and made an equitable " *arrangement* " with
her creditors, capitalising the amount of interest
then unpaid, and giving in exchange for the so-much
abused coupons, other stock bearing a gradually increasing interest, which has ever since been punc-
tually paid. The general public in England
apparently knows nothing of the settlement that
was made by Spain at that date, for people continue
to speak of overdue *coupons* in the same terms as
before, but in reality a very great distinction does
exist, and in Spain it is considered that an unfair
agitation has been kept up England after the whole
question was set at rest more than eight years ago.

The arrangement alluded to formed one part only

of the law of August 1st, 1851, by which a complete settlement was made on a new basis of all the debts of the state which were then in a very complicated condition.

Upwards of a hundred different descriptions of stock, representing more than 150 millions sterling, were then converted into three classes of paper, called consolidated, deferred, and redeemable debt, and the settlement it involved, providing as it did for the future payment of interest on all the existing loans, satisfied everybody excepting the holders of the overdue coupons. Spain, as I have said before, was not attempting to pay off all her creditors in full, which the state of her finances would not have allowed, but she *resumed payment* of the interest on that portion of her public debt, on which the coupons had remained unpaid, on what was considered the most favourable terms that her resources would permit, and in order to apply to the purpose not only the means then at her disposal, but also the increasing resources of the country, the principle was adopted of paying interest by a gradually increasing scale, first at 1 per cent., and eventually (after adding a quarter per cent. every two years), at the end of 18 years at the current rate of her consolidated fund, which is 3 per cent.

With regard to the interest which had accrued during the before mentioned period, when it had remained so long unsettled, the Spanish Government proposed that it should be capitalised and exchanged for the new "deferred stock" at one half of its nominal value. In other words, a *coupon*, which was worth on the Stock Exchange at that time (see "*Times*," July 1st, 1851) 8¾ per cent. of its nominal value, was to be exchanged for an inscription of the new stock worth nominally 50, and saleable at that time for about 20, and now for 33½ of its nominal value.*

This compromise which she proposed to her creditors, Spain thought *equitable*, because she gave them in exchange for their coupons something which was worth a good deal more than the market value of their bonds, but the English bondholders were not satisfied because they naturally considered themselves entitled to a payment in full of all the overdue interest.

Meetings were accordingly held in the City of London by the holders of the coupons, at which the subject was several times discussed, and it is difficult to say whether it was eventually agreed to accept the proposal or not. The last meeting, previous to the passing of the law, was held on the 3rd July, 1851, and resolutions were submitted by the Chairman which embodied a refusal of the terms, but in the report of the proceedings it is stated that—" These " resolutions were opposed by Mr. Crook and Mr. " Mocatta, the former stating that he considered it

---

* Many purely Spanish claims were at the same time recognised, and in exchange for them, a stock called " Redeemable," bearing *no interest*, was given to the claimants, which is gradually being paid off by yearly instalments.

" prudent to accept the proposal under protest, and
" the latter intimating that it was an irregular pro-
" ceeding on the part of the Committee to call the
" present meeting, when the bondholders possessed
" the opportunity of accepting or rejecting the
" terms offered as they might individually think fit
" under the decree brought forward." Baron L.
Rothschild, a member of the Committee, altogether
dissented from his colleagues, and " advised the
adoption of Bravo Murillo's decree." [*Times*, July
4th, 1851.]

This meeting, after a stormy discussion, ultimately
adopted a resolution, agreeing to " refer the whole
" matter back to the Committee, to take such steps
" as they might think proper to bring this long
" pending question to a satisfactory issue, alike
" honourable and creditable to Spain and beneficial
" to her creditors."

A few weeks later the law was passed by the
Spanish Cortes, the English bondholders intervened
in the conversion, and in exchange for the coupons
took inscriptions in the new deferred stock, upon
which the interest has been received by them ever
since, but they maintain that this settlement was
not final, insomuch as they duly protested against
its being considered so, and by this means reserved
their rights in respect to the liquidation of their
claims at the full nominal value of the coupons. It
ought, however, to be mentioned as somewhat important, that this protest was not signed in London

until the 3rd of December, more than three months after the law was passed.

A constant agitation has been kept up ever since. Transactions in any Spanish securities, issued since the date of this law, were prohibited on the Stock Exchanges of London and Amsterdam, thereby causing an incalculable injury to the mercantile interests of Spain; and the bondholders, assuming that only one-half of the debt had been liquidated, " issued certificates to represent the parties entitled " to the other half, whenever the liquidation thereof " may be made."

There is only one other point to which we need allude. It has been often stated that the settlement in question was forced upon the bondholders ; but this assertion is contradicted both by the statement of Mr. Mocatta, copied above from the City Article of the *Times* of July, 1851, and also by the recently published document, in which it is distinctly stated by the aforesaid Committee, that " by this " decree the Cortes *offered payment* of one-half of " the amount of the said arrears in certain bonds, " and cancelled the other half."

In Spain it is universally believed that this settlement of the, to them, very disagreeable coupon question ought, in justice, to be considered final, as it was intended to be. They say that a definite arrangement, proposed for acceptance or rejection was assented to by the English creditors, and their acceptance subsequently confirmed by the receipt of interest on the stock tendered to them in lieu of their claims. They deny *in toto* the competency of the bondholders, by means of a protest, to reserve a right to *some other settlement* whilst practically accepting that which was offered to them.

Now, it is not our object to examine whether Spain or her foreign creditors are, in point of law, in the right on this question; but, at any rate, there can be no doubt that the object of the former, in 1851, was worthy of a very different treatment from that which it has received. The English bondholders maintain that the settlement of this question (which would not involve the payment of more than £1,000,000) would cause a rise of at least 10 per cent. in the Spanish funds, and that thereby the country would be an immediate gainer to the extent of £15,000,000, besides the immense advantage which would indirectly accrue to her from the fact that such a measure would re-establish her credit on a level with that of the other first-rate powers in Europe; but if they imagine that Spain can be driven to a settlement of their claim because of its expediency, without her reason being first convinced of its justice, it is much to be feared that they will find themselves mistaken.

A Minister who took such a view in 1853 was universally supposed to be bribed, and his proposal to modify the law of 1851, on the score of expediency, caused the downfall of the Government to which he belonged.

Again, if any injustice *was* committed by the Spanish Government in 1851, it is not known to the nation at large, to whom mercantile or financial questions are, generally speaking, quite unfamiliar; and it is therefore not only unjust, but useless, to stigmatize the whole people for a fault which, moreover, would not in any case justify the offensive expressions which have been applied to it, as any one who has read the foregoing account will perceive. It might be well to remember the often repeated remark of the clever author of the " Handbook for Spain." The Spaniards may be led by a straw, but they are not to be driven by a rod of iron; and in no country is more to be obtained by the cheap outlay of courtesy in manner and speech—" *Cortesia* " *deboca mucho vale y poco cuesta.*"

Having now fully explained the nature of the arrangement entered into by Spain with her foreign creditors in 1851, which we think ought to be sufficient to modify in some degree the present state of hostility against Spain which exists very generally amongst mercantile men in this country, we will return to the subject of the war.

Their possessions on the coast of Morocco have always been regarded as of considerable importance by the Sovereigns of Spain, and for many years an hereditary war was kept up with the Moors, who made incessant attacks on them, especially on Ceuta and El Peñon.

Ceuta was taken from the Moors by John I. King of Portugal, in 1415, and passed into the hands of the Spaniards on the subjugation of Portugal by Philip II., in 1580. It is a town of about 10,000 inhabitants, and contains a cathedral, the bishop of which is suffragan to the Archbishop of Seville, besides several other large buildings, and a small harbour; but it is as a military and convict station that it is chiefly important. It is strongly fortified and surrounded by a high wall, and is built at the foot of the Monte de Hacho, the ancient Abila, one of the pillars of Hercules, and exactly opposite to Gibraltar, which is built on the other pillar.

In 1694 it was besieged by the Sultan Muley Ismael, to whom large subsidies were granted by Louis XIV. in order to enable him to carry on the war with vigour. It is said that in one attack alone, in 1696, the Moors lost 15,000 men; but although unsuccessful, they did not abandon the enterprise, and the siege lasted for 24 years longer. It has been since then several times attacked by the Africans, but never with any success.

Peñon de Velez is a fortified town, standing on a lofty rock, about eighty miles to the east of Ceuta, and also on the north coast of Morocco. It is built in the form of an amphitheatre, with two principal streets, and contains several churches, a bomb proof magazine, store houses, and a state prison. It was founded by Pedro of Navarre, captured by the Moors in 1522, but recovered in 1664 by the Spaniards, who have since retained it.

Melilla and Alhucema are small seaport towns, with well-fortified penal establishments further to the east. All these places are situated in the midst of the Riffian territory. Peñon de Velez and Alhucema are actually on the coast of the province of Al Riff; Ceuta and Melilla in the neighbouring provinces of Hasbat and Garet, and, owing to their situation, they have been exposed to the constant attacks of the Riff pirates, from whose depredations the vessels of France and Prussia have also suffered continually. In 1856 the French Government obtained compensation from Morocco for outrages committed by the pirates; but it was the first instance of such redress being peaceably granted, and France had previously taught the Sultan to respect her, by destroying his army at Isly, bombarding Tangiers, and occupying Mogadore. Prussia, on the other hand, allowed a Prince of royal blood to be attacked and ignominiously treated by these Riffians, without apparently thinking it in her power to obtain any redress.

Vessels belonging to Spain have been frequently attacked; on more than one occasion her subjects have been captured by the pirates, and it may be remembered that a few years ago accounts were published even in the English papers of the barbarous treatment to which some Spaniards were sub-jected during their captivity; but although in Spain great indignation was expressed, and the Sultan of Morocco was applied to in order that such outrages might be put a stop to, it has never been possible for Spain to obtain any redress.

As long ago as 1854 war between the two countries was spoken of, and again about two years later it was looked upon at Madrid as almost inevitable; but the Government of Spain was very unwilling to come to so serious a determination. At length, however, the attacks on Ceuta and the prevarications of the Moroccan Minister have occasioned an outbreak of hostilities, as has been already described in General O'Donnell's own words.

Its great popularity with the Spanish nation, and especially with the liberal party, is due to a variety of circumstances.

In the first place there is no doubt that it was imagined when the war was first spoken of that it was one which would have been generally approved of by other countries; the extirpation of the barbarous hordes of Riff pirates is a subject that had been often proclaimed to be highly desirable by our press as well as by their own; and, no European interests being involved, it was expected that Spain would be allowed this opportunity of proving to the world that she is not fallen so low as has so often been asserted of late years by some French and English writers.

Again, the feud which for centuries existed between Spaniards and Moors adds considerably to
the importance of the war in the eyes of the people,
and proud as they justly are of the present efficiency
of their army, it was believed by Spaniards that
England and France would offer no opposition to
a fair fight between Moors and Christians, and be
glad to look on and admire their chivalry.

Least of all was any opposition from England
anticipated, and it was even imagined by those who
hoped that the war would lead to an acquisition of
territory, that England would be far from feeling
dissatisfied at seeing a limit put by such means to
any further French encroachments on the frontiers
of Morocco. With Ceuta and three other fortresses
on the northern coast already in her possession,
Spain could not well "endanger the free navigation
of the straits" by an acquisition of further territory;
but whilst Tangiers remains in the hands of its present owners, it will always be subject to a sudden
seizure by France, who has of late years found it by
no means difficult to quarrel with the Sultan, and
has not hitherto thought it requisite to consult other
European governments when helping herself to a
slice of African territory.

We believe, however, that the Spanish Government has not at any time contemplated a permanent
acquisition of territory, although there have doubtless been many persons in the country who have
expressed such a wish.

Lastly, there is another reason for the war being popular, and it is by no means the least important. It is believed that if once the public mind could be thoroughly engaged with an object of absorbing interest abroad, it would tend greatly to a cessation of the bitter party dissensions at home. The Marquis of Molins, an orator of the opposition and a much esteemed poet, expressed these views in the Senate a few days before the declaration of war : " Señor Sierra, he said, has asked why all this show of force? Wherefore this increase in our army? What mean all these preparations for war? I answer him that our history requires them of us, that they are intended to strengthen us abroad and to unite us at home. Can you not see that on the opposite shore to ours, wherever indeed Islamism still exists, in that land where our arms were formerly triumphant and the sword of Cisneros dazzled and conquered, nothing now remains but empty space, which is fast being occupied by French civilization ? Either we must fill that space, or others will do it instead, and all our history signalises Spain as the country which is destined to drive back the followers of the Prophet and to replace them. It is thus only that we can aspire to consideration abroad. Foreign nations will respect us when they see that we possess the power to sustain our national character ; they will respect us, for action is power, and power is credit, and credit is wealth. Would you wish for riches and leave injuries unavenged ? Not so indeed ! If we would be powerful, if we would be respected, it is necessary that as a nation we should show signs of vitality.

"And this is not all: not only shall we thus acquire distinction abroad, but even amongst ourselves we shall at the same time gain in reputation. Such is our character: whenever we have not had foreign wars to sustain we have been consumed with internal discord. Let us but have some great object on which all our energy may be concentrated, something which shall inflame the minds of all parties, and then you will see that the dissensions amongst us will vanish, and we shall become united and great and powerful.

"Now would you know what is the great object that is capable of inspiring such unanimity? It is the desire to see the banner of Castile float on the towers of Morocco, and to carry the light of the Gospel into Moorish cities. To those who in such a cause would dare to ask the consent of foreigners I would address one word more: England looks on from Gibraltar, France from Oran, and you are Spaniards. Fight a good fight, and you will conquer the consent of all! and perhaps some day it may be written of us in history that to Isabel I. was due the conquest of America, and Isabel II. contributed to the civilization of Africa."

In order to explain how so much importance should be attached to the war as a means of quelling internal disputes, it is necessary to refer shortly to the present state of parties in Spain.

After a succession of ultra *Moderado* Governments, always unconstitutional and sometimes despotic in their tendencies, in 1854, the reins of State had devolved upon a ministry, some of the members of which added the reputation of flagrant corruptibility to the other characteristics of their party, and the indignation which this belief created throughout the country can be easily understood by those who remember that one of the chief causes of the French revolution of 1848 was the discovery of the frauds committed by General Cubières, the Minister of Public Works, M. Teste, and others. For several years the existence of corruption and malversation in the public offices and establishments of Spain had been loudly proclaimed by the opposition deputies, and now the Senate took upon itself to oppose the Government on a question which proved their belief in those charges; the question of railway concessions having been the principal cause of these imputations, a project of law was introduced by the Opposition, and carried by a considerable majority, prohibiting the granting of any concessions for the future without a special act of the Legislature. Heretofore this power had been vested in the Minister of Public Works, who was the most obnoxious member of the Ministry. The Government of the Count of San Luis thereupon adopted the extraordinary expedient of closing the Cortes, and on some of the principal members of the Senate memorialising the Queen, and requesting that the Houses of Legislature might be re-opened and the San Luis Ministry replaced by others possessing the confidence of the country, the principal heads of the Opposition were ordered into exile. General O'Donnell, who was comprehended in this arbitrary mandate, refused to obey it, and remained concealed in Madrid for several months, notwithstanding the efforts of the police to discover his hiding place. During this time he was actively engaged in promoting a general rising against the Government, and towards the end of June, with the aid of General Dulce, at that time Inspector General of Cavalry, he succeeded in gaining over the greater part of the garrison of Madrid to his cause, and openly proclaimed his determination to turn out the San Luis Ministry. A military *pronunciamiento* took place on the 28th June; two or three days later General O'Donnell was attacked at Vicalvaro by the rest of the garrison under General Quésada, and although the result of the battle was doubtful, he found his force too weak to hold his position in the immediate neighbourhood of Madrid, and retired to Aranjuez; and a few days later, having been pursued by the Minister of War, General Blaser, at the head of about 6000 men, he retreated slowly along the main south road until near Seville.

General O'Donnell, though himself a Moderado,

would not in such a cause make this an obstacle to such a coalition as would benefit the country, and consequently made overtures to the Progresista party, and at Manzanares, a few leagues south of Aranjuez, issued a proclamation in accordance with this new phase of the revolution, declaring his objects to be the re-establishment of the constitution of 1837, the maintenance of the throne of Isabel II., with the banishment of the Queen-Mother, the re-organization of the National Guard, and above all things purity in the Administration.

All the principal towns in the country then gave in their adhesion to the *pronunciamiento,* and rose against the Government. A revolution in a progresista sense ensued, promoted by Espartero, and after a few days' severe fighting in Madrid, Espartero and O'Donnell were sent for by the Queen to form a new ministry.*

* In judging of that class of Spaniards from which the army is recruited, illustrations from the time of the civil war are not fair. Civil wars are always barbarously conducted, *even in England.* The following anecdotes prove that the lower classes in Spain of the present day are good humoured, high bred, and noble fellows, besides being by nature generous foes.

The revolution commenced on the night of the 17th of July, with an attack by an armed mob on the houses of the Ministers, and of a few other obnoxious personages. The writer of these pages was standing near the house of the Count of San Luis, whose furniture formed a bonfire in the street, together with the well-known historian and Arabic scholar, Don Pascual Gayangos, when a voice was heard to cry, " From hence we go to Salamanca's." Immediately we together proceeded to that gentle-

From that moment General O'Donnell laboured
to form a party, to which the name was given of
the " Union-Liberal," in which it was his endeavour

man's house in order to warn him of the impending danger, and
having heard that he was already in hiding elsewhere, followed
him, received from him the keys of some important boxes, and
returned in time to enter at the same moment as the mob. Our
friend assisted Madame Salamanca to escape, and escorted her to
his own house, and we joined three or four gentlemen who were
known to us, who having come in with the crowd, were endeavour-
ing to dissuade them from sacking the house. In this they were
unsuccessful, for in a few minutes a simultaneous attack was made
on some large mirrors, and the crash of the falling glass served
as a signal to several hundred men who at once commenced hurling
magnificent furniture, heaps of plate and splendid paintings into
the street below. It seemed useless to withstand the mob any
longer, and the few respectable people who were amongst them
withdrew. Presently however the writer determined to return
alone in the vague hope of saving something from the fury of the
people. The house contained amongst other things a choice col_
lection of old paintings, and we hoped that some might yet be
rescued from destruction.

We found that part of the house had not yet been entered by
the mob, and stationing ourselves at the door leading to these
apartments, we managed to persuade four or five men to back us,
and for a long time kept the crowd from entering without much
difficulty. The person of an Englishman, "a guest in the country,"
was sufficient protection against any violence even from a lawless
rabble. Soon, however, the rest of the house was gutted, and
many hundreds of people, men and women, some wild with drink,
and all intensely excited with the mischief they were about, pressed
hard upon us, and we prepared to give way, when a voice whispered
in our ear, " say this part of the house is yours !" We hesitated,
and the brave young fellow relieved us from the necessity of
uttering this untruth. " Señores," he shouted, " here you cannot

to unite all the most moderate members of the different parties in the state. Espartero remained President of the Council until July 1856, by which

pass; beyond these doors are the apartments of this gentleman, he is a stranger, an Englishman, his person and his property are alike sacred by the laws of hospitality!" All those who heard him acquiesced at once, and they prepared to leave. Presently, however, the screams of the servants inside warned us that a door which we had overlooked had been forced open by another portion of the mob, and, accompanied by our new friend, we hurried to oppose their entrance. A considerable number of ruffians had already forced their way into some of the rooms, and were engaged in rifling drawers and closets; it seemed a very critical moment, but even with these violent and excited men my friend's argument, coupled with a determined attitude, was irresistible, and they ceased to plunder as soon as they could be induced to believe that an Englishman was the sufferer.

The mob left the house just in time to avoid bloodshed, for in less than half an hour after their departure a detachment of soldiers arrived, and the writer with his five or six comrades, who still remained in Mr. Salamanca's house, very narrowly escaped being shot as "leaders of the rabble!"

During the two succeeding days there was fighting in all parts of Madrid, but towards the afternoon of the second day a bugleman ran through the streets announcing a suspension of hostilities for half an hour. We took advantage of the truce to hasten to the Carrera de San Geronimo, where the fighting had been the hottest. A few hundred soldiers and civil guards who occupied the windows on one side of the street were capitulating, and a dense mass of people was calling on them clamorously from below to surrender unconditionally. The crowd was almost entirely composed of men who for the last thirty-six hours had been engaged in deadly combat with the soldiers, and there were many who were exasperated by the loss of comrades who had fallen by their side. The soldiers not unnaturally, therefore, feared to surrender their

time, he had not only exhausted the extraordinary
popularity which he had possessed two years before,
but he had come to be almost universally regarded as
totally devoid of talent as a statesman, and far too
weak for his position. A quarrel having ensued
between O'Donnell and one of the ministers named
Escosura, the cause of the latter was hotly espoused
by Espartero, who inconsiderately pushed matters
to such extremes that his continuance at the head of
the Government became impossible. When matters
were seen to be so serious, the Queen entreated him

arms. " They could not venture," they said, " to proceed through
the streets without their side arms." The mob settled the question
delightfully. As soon as it was plain to them what the difficulty
was, they made a rush into the houses, some by the doors and
some clambering through the upper windows, and emerged again
after a few moments with the enemy in their hands. Already
however every sign of enmity had disappeared, and in order that
the civil guards and soldiers should be perfectly safe from any
attack in the streets, they were escorted to their barracks by the
very men who a few minutes before were opposed to them, and who
now overwhelmed them with praises for the gallant resistance they
had made.

A very little while later the people heard with delight that Espartero had been sent for, and the fighting ceased; but his arrival
having been delayed for a fortnight they in the mean time held
their posts at the barricades, and spent an immensity of labour in
decorating them with flowers and trees, and with the portraits of
the Queen and the two heroes of the Revolution, Espartero and
O'Donnell. Chairs were placed under the shade of the trees, and
the sound of music and dancing was daily to be heard wherever
there was a barricade.

to discard Escosura, and to reform the Ministry with General O'Donnell, but his waning influence had made him so jealous of the latter, that nothing would satisfy him but O'Donnell's dismissal, and on that being shown to be impossible, he with great precipitation retired from the Ministry.

What then ensued was extraordinarily misunderstood by the English public.

Espartero's supporters were by this time limited to the extreme Liberals and the Republicans, and some of these hot-headed men were determined to resist the establishment of the new Government; for a few hours the attitude of a small number of deputies made it appear as if their resistance would be countenanced by the revolutionary part of the Cortes, and under these circumstances, the fierce red Republican, Sisto Camara, who commanded a battalion of militia—known as the most disorderly in the whole National Guard—was easily enabled to cause a collision with the troops, which was followed by several hours of street fighting between the militia and the army. The National Guards dispersed as soon as they had had time for a little reflection, but Pucheta, the bull-fighter, at the head of a few hundred rabble, kept the military at bay all that afternoon, and for several hours of the next day.

Espartero was very much blamed for not having prevented the bloodshed by a simple address to the nation, but it was supposed that he expected to be forced back to his post of Prime Minister on the shoulders of the people, forgetting, or not comprehending, that the two preceding years had made a complete change in his position. The hopes of the Liberal party in 1854 were centered in him as their acknowledged head, but whatever he might have been at that time, years and illness, added to the responsibilities of office, had by 1856, so weakened his faculties that he had brought the country almost to a state of anarchy, and had entirely lost the confidence of the most temperate of his supporters.

Unfortunately the representative of England (the ever to be regretted Lord Howden) was absent from Spain at this time, and the great authority with the public, the *Times'* "own correspondent," had been withdrawn from Madrid some time before, when Espartero's utter incapacity for governing was not yet suspected, and he was still the idol of the people and the recognised chief of the Liberal party. Accordingly his fall was perhaps not unnaturally misunderstood, and was looked upon as the downfall of liberty, and triumph of a reactionary party, and the impression created in England by the events I have recorded was exceedingly unfavourable to O'Donnell. It was even at first reported that the Constitution was to be trampled under foot, and that the Cortes had assembled at Saragossa to resist the new Government at the head of an indignant people, the Queen was described as false and treacherous, and O'Donnell was supposed to be a

merciless foe of the Liberal party, which it was said
he was bent only on destroying !

It is of no little importance to rectify the mistake
that was then committed by the English public, for
even the " Annual Register," from which future
historians will doubtless cull much of the information
with which to compile the chronicles of Spain, was
completely misled, and represents what passed at
that time as " the overthrow of constitutional liberty
in Spain," adding a rebuke to the Paris *Moniteur*
for taking an entirely different view of what had
passed.

At the same time, we cannot say that it is very
surprising that some mistakes should have been
made in England, for even in Spain itself there were
many people who mistrusted O'Donnell, and it was
not until after an interregnum of a few months,
during which time General Narvaez reigned in
his stead, that the party of the " *Union-Liberal* "
(which may be called the Liberal Conservative)
determined to give him their decided support.

General O'Donnell has doubtless had a most difficult part to play, but he deserves the greatest credit
for the way in which he has performed it.

He has succeeded in forming a powerful and
highly respected party, out of very discordant ele-
ments, and in the face of an opposition from the
most important leaders of the old parties of extreme
Moderados, Polacos, Bravo Murillistas, &c. (La Liga)
who boast that they monopolise all the chief states-

craft in the kingdom. He is now supported by all the most moderate men, both amongst the Progresistas and Moderados; and, although doubtless the most numerous, the former party were so greatly wanting in statesmen of repute, that the coalition is one of incalculable advantage to them.

Amongst the Liberals a few individuals only, whose personal friendship for Espartero has made it difficult for them to coalesce with the new leader (Olozoga, Escosura, Calvo Asensio), still hold aloof on general questions, and have formed a separate party which goes by the name of *Los Puros* (the Radicals), but on the question of the war, they support General O'Donnell, so that at this moment the desired effect appears to have been already partly produced, and the Liberals are strong and united.

All O'Donnell's acts have been strictly in conformity with constitutional practices, the Administration is purified of its former corruption, and his financial measures have been most successful.

The advance in wealth and general prosperity which has been made by Spain during the last few years, and especially since 1854, has indeed been extraordinary; and Europe has been not a little surprised, on the war with Morocco breaking out, to learn, not only that she is now rich and prosperous, but that she has a large army at her disposal, and even a considerable navy also. Her troops, it is found, are armed with Minié rifles, and more than half the artillery is composed of rifled cannons whilst she has shown that she has the means of transporting an army of 50,000 men to the coast of Africa, with 80 pieces of cannon and a battering train, besides munitions of war and provisions for an expedition which is equal in numbers to that which England and France first landed in the Crimea.

Moreover, it appears that the expenses of the war are not only not to be met by a loan, but the only alteration in the ordinary taxation which the Finance Minister has thought it necessary to demand, is an addition to the tax on real property of 12 per cent of its present amount, and of 10 per cent to the ordinary octroi duties, and the taxes on trades and on mortgages; with a deduction from the salaries of Government employés, and all classes whose incomes are derived from the State, not to exceed 8 per cent on salaries of from £30 to £150 sterling per annum, or 10 per cent on those exceeding £150 per annum.

The clergy, army and navy, and collectors of the revenue, were exempted by the law from the effects of this tax on incomes, but the clergy and many officers have spontaneously declined the exemption. The remainder of the funds are to be provided by applying to the purpose whatever amount may be found requisite out of the sum of £20,000,000 which was voted by the Cortes at the commencement of this year for increasing the military and naval defences of the country and for other public works, payable out of the proceeds of the sale of national property.

The fact that Spain is undertaking an important foreign war without having recourse to a loan is very remarkable. There is indeed no other country in Europe whose revenue has made so marked a progress during the last ten years as has that of Spain. In 1848 it amounted to about £12,000,000 sterling, in 1854 it was between 14 and 15,000,000, whilst in 1858 it exceeded £20,000,000 !

The expenses of the Government have not very much increased, and by an examination of the subjoined table it will be seen that she has now an amount of disposable revenue after paying the interest on her debt, which, if compared with her population, is only exceeded by that of France and of England, whilst the expense of her army and navy has been hitherto comparatively insignificant as compared with theirs.

France has 27 $\frac{44}{100}$ shillings of disposable revenue per head of population.

England	25 shillings	,,	,,
Spain	23 ,,	,,	,,
Prussia	19 $\frac{44}{100}$,,	,,	,,
Holland	19 $\frac{37}{100}$,,	,,	,,
Russia	12 $\frac{28}{100}$,,	,,	,,
Austria	10 $\frac{32}{100}$,,	,,	,,

The sale of national property, the extension of railways, the improvement in the national education of the people, and many other recent laws which have been the results of the revolution of 1854, are all measures tending to increase this state of pros-

perity. It is remarkable that, whilst at the commencement of this century only 1 in 340 were edu-
cated, now it is calculated that to every 1 in 17 the
means of elementary schooling is afforded. Railways are being constructed in all directions, princi-
pally with the aid of French companies, as our own
capitalists are virtually excluded by the act of the
Stock Exchange, to which we have before alluded;
the greater part of the necessary capital is however
found in Spain, as the Government grants very
considerable subventions, and the provincial authorities are enabled to subscribe largely to them by
applying to the purpose the funds now obtainable by
the sale of national property.

In 1855 the law of *Desamortizacion* was passed,
under which the whole of the land held in mort-
main by the State, the Church, and certain other
corporations is being sold to individual purchasers;
its operation was afterwards suspended, owing to the
opposition that it encountered from the clerical
party, until the consent of the Pope could be obtained to the disposal of the property which was
dependant on the Church authorities; but now it is
again in full force with the approbation of all parties. By this law the provincial authorities are
allowed to invest 80 per cent. of the produce of the
sales of their lands in works of public utility; and
the favourable terms which have been established,
have induced so great a number of purchasers to
present themselves whenever an auction takes place,

that, on an average, the land has sold for three times the amount which it was originally supposed it would fetch; the payments extend over a term of 14 years, so that their annual produce when brought into cultivation in many cases more than pays the purchase money, and it is estimated that by this means a sum of nearly £60,000,000 sterling will become available for public works in the course of the next 20 years, the greater part of which will be laid out on railways.

This will be a source of incalculable wealth to Spain, and the fact of such an immense extent of land* hitherto sterile being thus brought into cultivation is likely to have nearly an equal degree of influence on the increasing prosperity of this country.

We subjoin a tabular statement of the vessels of war which have been constructed during the reign of the present Queen, and it will be seen that these vessels alone form a steam flotilla of considerable importance.

The tonnage of her mercantile navy has more than doubled since 1849, and her commerce increased in a still greater proportion.

We see then that Spain may not without reason be anxious to occupy more attention, and may con-

* We know of one such district belonging to a municipal corporation, which is upwards of one million acres (1600 square miles) in extent, and yet does not produce a thousand pounds per annum.

sider herself entitled to hold a higher place in the councils of Europe than has of late years been allotted to her; and it will not appear strange that such an enthusiastic and highly chivalrous people should rejoice at the opportunity being offered to them of proving the advance made by their country by the indirect means of a war, in which their cause is both just and reasonable, and no European interests are imperilled, whilst in this cause their soldiers are at the same time called upon to do combat with mussalmans and barbarians in a country which, if ever enlightened, must become so by the introduction of Christianity and European civilization.

England justifies to herself her immense Asiatic conquests on no other plea, and surely she need not regard with any jealousy the efforts of a rival in the great cause of African civilization.

Let it also be borne in mind that in Spain itself there is yet a struggle going on between the party which represents constitutional liberty and that of arbitrary governments. The first is the cause of England throughout the world, and in Spain it is at this moment represented by O'Donnell and the army in Africa. To be prosperous, and great, and free, Spain requires only a united Liberal party and a strong Government, and such objects may fairly enlist the sympathies of Englishmen.

The idea that has in some quarters become prevalent in England, that the war has been undertaken at the instigation of France, is contrary to the whole spirit of the people. A few months ago there was no country in Europe more ready to side with England in case of a general war, which was then thought probable, for such is indeed the traditional policy of the liberal party in Spain. It will be wholly our own fault if she is driven to an alliance with France.

Let us therefore conclude with an appeal to that great engine of public opinion—the Press of England—to watch with a more friendly feeling the aspirations of a people which, though of late years they have fallen a little behind us in wealth and commercial prosperity, is a great nation, an old ally of England, and worthy in very many respects of our admiration and esteem.